© 1997 Franklin Watts

Franklin Watts
96 Leonard Street
London EC2A 4RH

Franklin Watts Australia
14 Mars Road
Lane Cove
New South Wales

ISBN: 0 7496 2619 4

Dewey Classification 728

© Illustrations 1997
Luigi Galante & Simone Boni

Written by
Nicola Baxter

Concept and design by
Eljay Yildirim

Edited by
Kyla Barber

Architectural Consultant
Paul Davies

**Many thanks to Janet Ball,
Tom Williamson and Satoshi
Kitamura for their help and advice.**

A CIP catalogue record for this book
is available from the British Library

Printed in Italy

INSIDE STORY
~ *Extraordinary Buildings Unfolded* ~

Written by Nicola Baxter

Illustrated by Luigi Galante & Simone Boni

Contents

FRANKLIN WATTS
NEW YORK • LONDON • SYDNEY

A House or a Home?

What is a home? It can be a castle or a cottage, a palace or an apartment. Through the centuries, people have lived in many different kinds of building as advances in technology have changed the way we live – and the homes we live in. When candles first took the place of flaming torches, what a difference it made to smoke-filled rooms! Now, electricity seems the only choice for lighting. Of course, the reasons *why* we need homes are the same as in the earliest times. A home shelters us from cold and heat, from the wind and the wet. It is a safe place to sleep and somewhere to spend time with family and friends. But homes say more about us than that. After all, if all homes have the same purpose, why don't they look more alike?

First impressions

The very first glimpse of a building can tell us a great deal. Were its owners wealthy or poor? Did they build to impress, like a Count in a French château, or to keep out their enemies, like a Baron in a Norman castle. Did they expect to live quietly and privately, or to entertain guests at lavish parties? Or maybe, like a Sultan in a Moorish palace, they were much more interested in the *inside* of their home than the outside.

Left: The simplicity of the interior of a Japanese palace at once creates a feeling of peace and harmony. It has been built to allow cool air to circulate freely.

The builders of the Norman castle below had no way of calculating how thick the walls should be. They hoped for the best and relied upon their experience of building huge cathedrals. Only the power of the people's faith in God or their fear of the King could harness the labour needed for such enormous undertakings.

Moorish builders knew much more about engineering and design. They were good at mathematics and had been perfecting the same styles for centuries. By working with small units, fitted together in a many different ways, they created intricate and beautiful mosques and palaces that could be expanded and altered over the years.

Japanese builders had few concerns about supporting the weight of a structure, but they believed that everything should be as simply and perfectly made as possible. Aiming for a sense of oneness (or unity) with the natural world, they created homes and palaces using only bamboo, wood, reeds and paper.

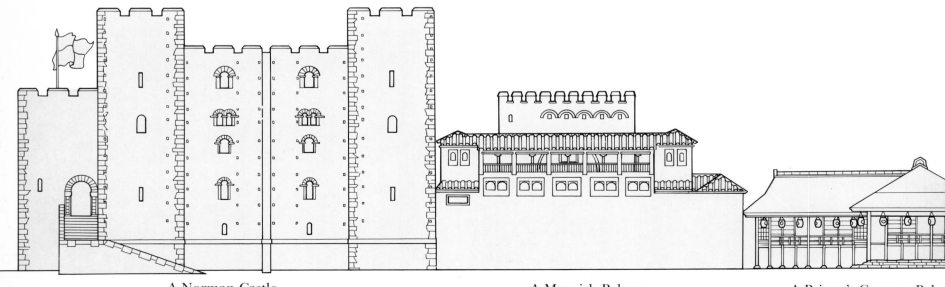

A Norman Castle
page 4

A Moorish Palace
page 8

A Prince's Country Pala
page 12

HOW WAS IT BUILT?

Just as new technology has changed the things inside our homes, it has also changed the way houses are built. Castle builders had to shape each piece of stone by hand. Hundreds of workers were needed. Later, bricks were machine made. One bricklayer could lay hundreds in a single day. In the twelfth century, only someone as powerful as a medieval Baron could afford to have stone brought from many miles away at a time when travelling was still far from easy. In the Victorian era, trains and canals made it cheap and easy to bring slate from Wales to roof the homes of London. When traditional building materials were unavailable, eighteenth-century American builders found ways to carve walls made of wood so that they *looked like* stone!

HOMEWORK

Even after a home has been built, the work is not over. Someone must keep it clean and in good repair. Housekeeping has changed over the years too. In a French château in the seventeenth century, few people minded if things were dirty, so long as they *looked* attractive. A thin veneer, or splash of powder and perfume were enough to create the desired appearance. But for the Victorians, cleanliness was next to godliness – everything had to be spotless, even those things that were out of view! Today, vacuum cleaners and washing machines make it much easier to keep things looking spick and span. In the past, an army of servants or slaves worked from dawn until dusk to keep dust at bay – but only if the homeowners were wealthy enough to afford them.

HOME VISITS

The amazing thing about homes, whenever they were built or wherever they are, is that it doesn't matter how often you turn back to them, there is always something new to look at. Explore the homes shown on these pages, then read about the people who lived in them. Find out about the styles and materials that were used, and identify the fashions and trends. Then revisit the buildings – and try to spot all the features that you have read about. These houses reveal more about their occupants than you would ever imagine!

A French aristocrat needed a show house: to let everyone know that he appreciated and could afford the best of everything. He borrowed classical styles from past civilizations that he admired – pillars from the Greeks and carvings from the Romans – to decorate his luxurious home.

Even after America gained independence from Britain, its builders still looked to Europe for ideas. But by using different materials and incorporating their own styles, they designed buildings that still look unmistakably American today, both inside and out, creating a new style for a new beginning.

The Victorians were able to build huge numbers of homes very quickly by using identical plans and factory-made materials. Row after row of homes looked similar on the outside, but inside, they were packed with heavy furniture and ornaments, so that no two homes could ever look the same.

In America, after the Second World War, many people enjoyed a new prosperity. They could afford modern homes with all the latest electrical gadgets that saved hours of painstaking work. The days when a dozen servants were needed for a few people to live a life of comfort were gone for ever.

An Aristocrat's Château
page 16

A Plantation House
page 20

A Victorian Town House
page 24

An American Apartment Block
page 28

A NORMAN CASTLE
England 1160

Straightening his aching back in the stony field, the first thing the serf sees, towering above him, is the Baron's massive castle. It is a constant reminder that less than a hundred years ago, in 1066, William, Duke of Normandy, seized the English throne at the Battle of Hastings and changed the country forever.

The King now on the throne of England has an entire country to control. He cannot do it alone. Instead, here, as in the rest of his kingdom, he has chosen a Baron to represent him. It is the Baron's job to keep the peace and dispense justice on the King's behalf.

FIRST A FORTRESS

These are troubled times. The Baron must be constantly prepared for an attack from home or abroad. The castle's walls are enormously thick, built to withstand battering rams and catapults. Inside the curtain wall, local people can gather for safety if danger comes. This building is a fortress first and a home second.

PRACTICAL AND PORTABLE

The Baron can never rest. When he has made sure that all is well here, he will be on his way to another castle or manor, to make his presence felt there. This castle will stand silent and empty, except for a skeleton staff. As it is not safe to leave valuables in the castle while the Baron is away, he will take his few possessions with him. The hangings on the walls can be taken down and rolled up. Small items can be packed into the chests that are also used for seating. Only beds and tables can safely be left behind, as tables are made simply from trestles with rough boards on top. The beds are also unfinished boards and posts, covered when in use by curtains and bedclothes. Sturdy mules will carry the Baron's luggage to his next resting place. There, it will be less than a day's work to unpack into his new temporary "home".

Above: The castle stands high, on a manmade mound. A curtain wall is its first line of defence.

Below: Roads are bad and travel, even by horseback, is slow and dangerous. Men-at-arms guard the Baron and his valuables as he moves on to another of his manors.

DARKNESS AND DAMP

At this time of year, in the dark and draughty rooms, visitors are grateful for fires that blaze in the hearths and the flaming torches on the walls. But there is a price to pay. The castle's windows are small, designed to keep out enemy arrows and biting winds. Thick black smoke swirls through the rooms, covering walls and tables, clothes and faces with soot. Even this is preferable to the dampness and cold of the unheated, unlit passages – or the earthen-floored huts of the serfs outside the castle walls.

Left: Like most of the rooms in the castle, the great hall serves many purposes – meeting room, dining room and even, when the feasting is over for the night, bedroom!

A FEAST FOR FRIENDS

Tonight the Baron is entertaining local nobles to a feast in the great hall, to remind them that he is in charge! Later, the trestle tables will be pushed aside and most people will settle down to sleep on the hard floor. The Baron and his family are rather more comfortable on the floor above, where curtained beds offer a little privacy and some protection from the cruel draughts.

THE BARON'S MEN

The Baron cannot attend to every detail of this huge building. He has a team of officials and servants to make sure that everything runs smoothly.

The marshal, as rough and ready as the men he controls, is responsible for the horses, the garrison and the outside servants.

The Baron's family

Under the castellan's sharp eye, a well maintained castle is a strong castle. Local crafts-men have a job for life, slowly repairing the stone walls after a battering from enemy forces or the English weather!

The chamberlain makes sure that all the Baron's food and drink is tasted before it reaches his table. Before fridges, freezers or tin cans, food may easily be bad – and as the Baron is not a popular man there is always the chance that it has been poisoned!

The steward is the Baron's accountant and is almost as feared as his master. He makes sure that the lesser nobles and serfs pay what is due.

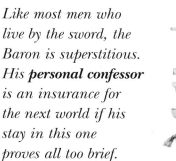

Like most men who live by the sword, the Baron is superstitious. His personal confessor is an insurance for the next world if his stay in this one proves all too brief.

For the Baron's men-at-arms, long stretches of boredom are broken only by brief periods of brutal activity. They must be ready at all times to fight for their Baron and their King.

FACTS & FEATURES

Location: the castle is built on a mound, so that enemies must attack uphill, at a disadvantage. But the mound is manmade and the massive weight of the castle may eventually cause it to subside.

Construction: builders at this time are not able to work out the stresses and strains that the castle's walls must bear. They simply continue by trial and error, hoping that by building massively thick walls, they can create a stable structure.

The keep: the strongest, central part of the castle.

Ashlar facing: the middles of the walls are made of rubble, but the outsides are covered with fine ashlar stone, brought at great expense from France.

Norman arches: the round arches above windows and doors, often with ornate carved decorations, are typical of this time and culture.

Spiral staircases: these narrow stairs wind clockwise, making it difficult for a right-handed attacker to use his sword as he climbs up.

Forebuilding: this covers over the entrance to the castle, making it easier to defend.

Washing and toilets: basic toilet arrangements make the lower floors of the castle particularly smelly and unhealthy. Water is drawn up from a well below the castle.

TODAY IN THE CASTLE...
TODAY TWO UNWISE THIEVES HAVE BEEN CAUGHT BY THE MEN-AT-ARMS AND ARE ON THEIR WAY TO THE DARKEST, MOST MISERABLE ROOM IN THE CASTLE. SOMEONE ELSE MAY END UP THERE TOO, IF HE HAS MUCH MORE OF THE BARON'S ALE!

A MOORISH PALACE
Spain 1400

Many palaces are built to impress. They dazzle the onlooker with the wealth and power of their owner. But in fifteenth-century Spain, the Sultan who owns this palace does not need to trumpet his importance. He is descended from the Moors who arrived from Africa over 600 years ago to conquer this part of Europe. Now, his city is the most civilized and luxurious in Europe. The Sultan follows the teachings of Islam and does not believe in a show of luxury. His home reveals the beauty of its rooms and courtyards only to those invited behind the high brick walls. For them, entering from the dusty street, the palace's flowers and fountains and sweet perfumes seem like a dream of paradise, as described in the Koran, the holy book of Islam.

Left: The Sultan is not often seen by ordinary people. His mystery is one of his most powerful weapons. Judges and administrators deal with disputes on his behalf, but he is the final court of appeal if agreement cannot be reached.

AT HOME IN THE HEAT
In a hot, dry land, it is not damp and cold that are the enemies, but heat and dust. The sun burns down day after day. This palace has small openings and intricately carved screens that allow cool air to flow through the building and prevent the merciless sun from fading the carpets and silk hangings inside.

THE WEALTH OF WATER
The Moors and the beliefs they follow come from a desert land, where water is infinitely more precious than gold. Piped into the palace, via an aqueduct from the river far below, water is not only used for drinking and bathing. The pools and fountains that please the eye and cool the air are a true luxury, reminding the faithful of God's gifts to them in this life and the promise of better things in the life to come.

Above: In the Islamic world, tradition is of great importance. The rich decorations of the graceful pillars, trellises and screens have not changed greatly over the centuries, but they have become finer and more elaborate.

Below: Even the flowers in the courtyards are planted in patterns as detailed as those on the traditional woven carpets.

A CITY STATE
All around the palace stretch flourishing fields of crops unknown in Europe before the Moors arrived. Rice, sugar-cane and cotton grow on the surrounding plains, watered by complex systems of irrigation. But it is the city that is the real heart of this civilization. Narrow winding streets, bustling with traders and craftsmen, lead to the palace walls. Inside, the engineering skills that bring water to the fields have created a tranquil garden retreat, seconds from the very heart of the Sultan's commercial empire.

Even in the heat of the day, fresh air flows from the water-cooled gardens, through the arches and trellises, into the rooms beyond. The palace is inward looking. There are few windows on the outer walls, only battlements patrolled by guards.

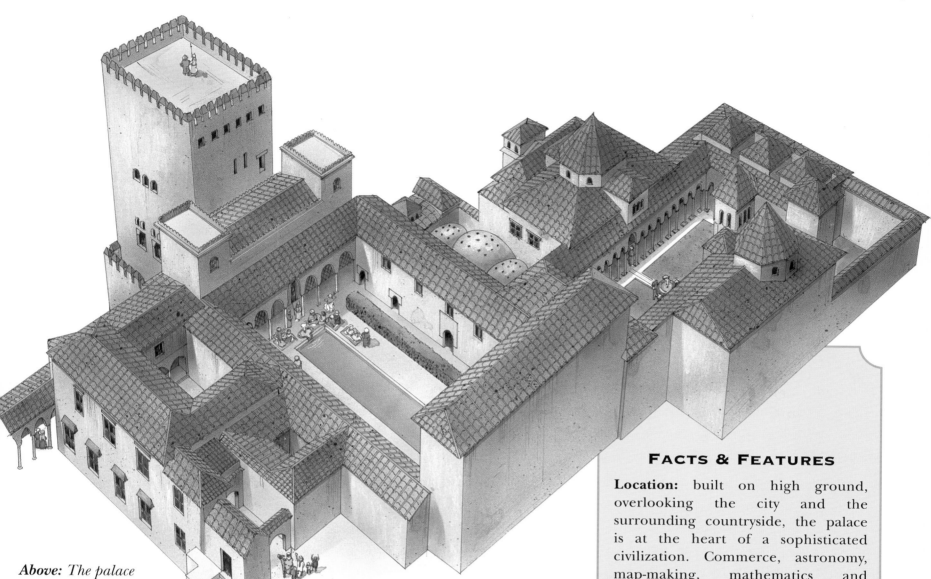

Above: *The palace unfolds from room to room and courtyard to courtyard, like a giant maze. At the centre, reached only by the privileged few, the Sultan leads his very private life. The plain curtain wall that surrounds the palace is all that is visible to the public at large, giving no hint of the wonders within.*

DUST TO DUST

Although the palace looks imposing, it is simply built from the earth on which it stands. Bricks and tiles are shaped from clay and left to dry in the hot sun. Repairs are easy as everything is made of small units that can be replaced. There are no enormous blocks of stone to manhandle. The same methods have been used for centuries. After a few years, it is very hard to see where repairs have been made, or new walls and courtyards built.

A PATTERNED PALACE

A palace like this has not been built to one grand plan. Rooms and courtyards have been added as modules, or sections, put together to create a larger whole. In a similar way, the patterns found on every surface, in carvings, coloured tiles, or woven silk, can be endlessly repeated and combined to make new and more intricate designs.

> TODAY IN THE PALACE...
> ISLAM ENCOURAGES ITS FOLLOWERS TO SHOW HOSPITALITY TO TRAVELLERS. TODAY, VISITORS ARE BEING OFFERED A FRUIT FROM THE EAST THAT WAS UNKNOWN IN EUROPE UNTIL THE COMING OF THE MOORS.
> TILED FLOORS ARE COOL IN A HOT CLIMATE BUT THEY ARE HARD TO SIT ON! IN FACT, VISITORS ARE RECLINING ON REAL WORKS OF ART, FOR WHICH ISLAMIC CRAFTSMEN ARE JUSTLY FAMOUS.

FACTS & FEATURES

Location: built on high ground, overlooking the city and the surrounding countryside, the palace is at the heart of a sophisticated civilization. Commerce, astronomy, map-making, mathematics and agriculture are all much more highly developed here in Islamic Spain than anywhere else in Europe.

Construction: the builders of this palace are highly skilled. They have learnt from experience how to develop arches and pillars so that heavy weights can be balanced on the very slenderest of supports.

Screens: divide spaces in this large building, whilst allowing cool air and light to filter through the decorative fretwork. The Sultan's wives, who live separately from the men, can view all the activities in the palace through the screens, but at the same time, remain modestly hidden themselves.

Alcoves: words such as alcohol and algebra have entered many languages from Arabic. "Alcove", also originally an Arabic word, means a shallow recess in a wall, which may be purely decorative or used to display special ornaments. Craftsmen in this city are highly skilled in creating beautiful objects of metal, wood and stone.

11

A PRINCE'S COUNTRY PALACE
Japan 1640

Left: *The design of the garden is as important as that of the palace. It is meant to be explored slowly, and is not intended to impress at first sight.*

The Prince who lives in this palace may have royal blood, but his life is as confined, in its way, as that of the poorest peasant. Now that the real power in the country has moved to the Shogun, the imperial court is a shadow of its former glory. But over his country home and its grounds, the Prince has exercised total control. Every stone and every twig has been positioned around the manmade lake by experts in garden design to create the desired effect. In his country retreat, the Prince dedicates his time to the pursuit of perfection in nature, in art and in thought.

A FABULOUS FARMHOUSE

At first sight, the palace appears to be as simple as any of the farmhouses in the surrounding countryside. Like them, it is made entirely of natural materials. Wood and bamboo form the structure and much of the interior decoration. Paper – made from vegetable materials – has been used to create screens and lanterns. The design seems straightforward. The roof beams are not hidden behind carving and decoration but are plain to see. A closer look, however, reveals that expert hands have been at work. Every surface is smooth and finished. Every joint is exquisitely made. The building methods may resemble those in lesser homes, but master craftsmen have been at work, directed by a man who knows exactly what effect he wishes to create for himself and his guests.

Below: Just as the Prince's favourite book describes, the boat boys wear Chinese costumes in colourful silks. From the Moon Viewing Platform of his home, the Prince can take in this tranquil evening and enjoy its perfection – after all, it is a scene he created.

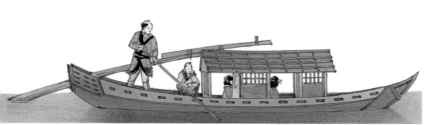

THIS EVENING IN THE PALACE...
THIS EVENING TWO MUSICIANS ENTERTAIN THE ASSEMBLED COMPANY.
THEIR DELICATE PLAYING IS UNLIKELY TO WAKE THE SLEEPING GUEST
WHO HAS JUST ARRIVED.
IN THE HEAT OF THE NIGHT, SOME GUESTS ARE USING TRADITIONAL
METHODS TO KEEP COOL.

Above: This family picture is a rare scene. A nobleman's life is usually spent apart from his wife and children, who live in their own, very different, world.

A HOMAGE TO THE PAST

The Prince is a cultured man. His country palace reflects his pleasure in reading and his enjoyment of looking back to the golden age of imperial life, five hundred years before. It is no accident that the garden resembles one described in a poem he particularly likes. The little boats on the lake copy those described in his favourite book. Here, he can surround himself with people who share his passion for tradition and art and who join him in the intricate and formal ritual of the tea-ceremony. He can enjoy the purity of nature, and see in the falling of a leaf the message that his own life may be as beautiful but brief.

FACTS & FEATURES

Location: the artful placing of wood and water, plants and stones has completely changed what was here before – it used to be a melon patch!

Construction: built on stilts, the palace avoids problems of damp and flooding. In hot weather, the air circulating under the building helps to keep the rooms above cool and fresh.

Lighting and heating: even in the depths of winter, the Prince can visit his palace, warmed by hot coals in special containers. At night, paper lanterns give a glowing light. But the danger of fire is always present, as every part of the palace could burn to ashes in seconds.

Tatami mats: made of rice straw, cover the floors in the simplest way.

Paper screens: the same room may be used for many purposes – eating, sleeping or entertaining. Paper screens can be opened or closed to alter the size of the rooms and allow cooling breezes to sift through the house. But paper walls provide very little privacy. The formal rules of conduct and politeness are very necessary in so open an environment.

An Aristocrat's Château
France 1690

The passengers of a rattling horse-drawn coach on its way to Paris glimpse the château from their grimy window. They know at first glance that this is the home of a man of power and influence. And that is exactly what the Count intends. His family, friends, staff and important visitors can see at once that he is a wealthy man of the highest social position. The house is in the very latest style, showing that he has taste and learning. It is a fitting stage for the part that he plays among the most powerful people in the country.

FROM DEFENCE TO DISPLAY

The Count's family has lived on these lands for centuries now. To build his new château, the Count pulled down the earlier family home. That house looked back to a different age, when a landowner might need to defend his property. Today the Count has only to concern himself with improving his favoured position with King Louis XIV. It is the King who dispenses greater power and influence. Tonight the Count is specially favoured, for the King is visiting. Ever anxious to better his prospects, the Count has invited the great and the good to a glittering evening's entertainment. The magnificence of the evening is only possible with the help of literally hundreds of servants, who are vital to the running of the Count's lavish home and lifestyle.

The previous family home.

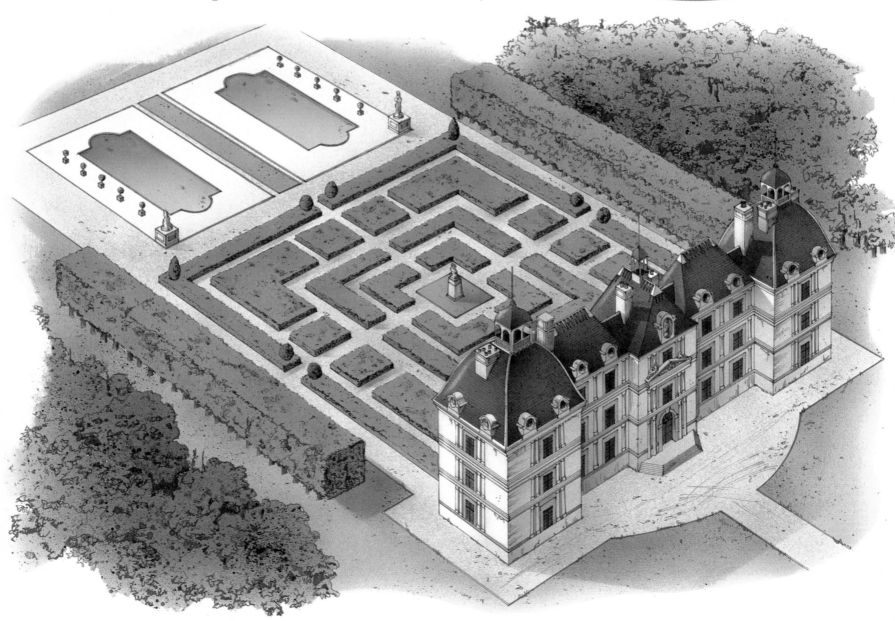

18

THE CORRIDORS OF POWER

There is no need in this extensive home for rooms to serve more than one purpose. Each is decorated in keeping with the activity it was designed for. Important family members and visitors live in apartments of three or four rooms. Only someone who is considered an equal or superior is invited to move through to the last, most private room. Those waiting in the outer rooms or the hall outside are made all too aware of their position in the scheme of things.

Above: The Count inherited his position from his father and has been working hard to improve it ever since. His arranged marriage into a wealthy family has helped. The Count's mother lives with him.

Above: The Count's and Countess's younger children are looked after by nursemaids at the top of the house. The older children are already learning how to take their proper place in society.

TONIGHT IN THE CHATEAU...
TONIGHT THE COUNT'S GUESTS ARE ENJOYING FOOD, MUSIC AND DANCING. BUT SOME OF THE SERVANTS ARE ALSO LETTING THEIR HAIR DOWN.
A FEW PEOPLE HAVE DECIDED TO ESCAPE THE CROWDS — SOME MAY EVEN HAVE AMOROUS INTENTIONS!

Above: This party provides an excellent opportunity to improve one's social position. The Count's brother-in-law hopes to arrange his daughter's marriage to a young man of good family. The Count's tutor may want to marry the daughter himself, but society's strict rules mean that they can never have a future together.

Above: The Count has thirty servants dressed in his own livery, or uniform. They show his power and influence simply by being there. Out of sight of the guests, dozens of other servants are hard at work preparing the food and wine, and helping the Count and his family get ready for the great party ahead.

A Plantation House
America 1797

A hero returns to the estate his family has owned for a hundred years to find that his home is sadly in need of some care and attention. Now that he has played his part in the bitter struggle for independence from Britain and the early days of the new government, the Landowner looks forward to his retirement. But it is unlikely to be a restful one. There is much to do to develop his house and grounds – and he is brimming with ideas!

Above: The Landowner has adopted the latest ideas from Europe, especially in his garden designs. As well as formal gardens, he has chosen areas to be laid out in a more natural way.

Below: The quarters for the ninety slaves who work in the house and grounds have been designed and built under the Landowner's supervision. Nevertheless, they are a great deal less comfortable than his own home.

A QUESTION OF CONSCIENCE

Ninety slaves work in the house, grounds and farm. The Landowner's life could not continue in this style if they did not. Almost all the work on the estate has to be done by hand. But although the Landowner lives in a world where slavery is very common and often accepted, he is no longer sure that it is right to buy and sell other human beings. He has left instructions in his will that "his" slaves are to be freed after his death. In the meantime, he tries to treat them well, having his own doctor look after them when they are ill and doing his best not to split up families, as so many other slave-owners do. In fact, the Landowner is unusual in his care for his workers, but while he has a choice of how he lives his life, they do not.

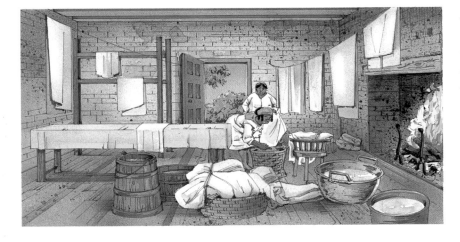

Left: *The plantation is as self-sufficient as a small village. It has its own weaver, shoemaker, carpenter and blacksmith, each housed in a specially built workshop. There are also a laundry, a bakery, a brewhouse, and a smokehouse.*

A WELCOME TO ALL

The Landowner is a hospitable man, welcoming visitors to his home. It is a custom that dates from the days when there were only scattered settlements in this land, and places to rest for the night were few and far between. But the house often becomes very crowded and guests overflow into the adjoining buildings. In the attics, the Land-owner's wife stores beds that can be assembled quickly when the rest of house is bursting at the seams.

FROM THE OLD TO THE NEW

Although the new country has freed itself from its European rulers, it is still to Europe that the Landowner looks for ideas about his home. He has many English books on gardens, architecture and farming and has supervised most of the improvements to the family home himself. Even today, in freezing weather, he was up before his managers, to make sure that a good day's work was done.

THIS MORNING IN THE HOUSE...
THIS MORNING THE FRONT OF THE HOUSE IS RECEIVING A MUCH-NEEDED COAT OF PAINT, BUT IT LOOKS AS THOUGH THE PORCH FLOOR MAY ACCIDENTALLY RECEIVE ONE TOO! IN THREE ROOMS OF THE HOUSE, FOUR-LEGGED FRIENDS ARE ABOUT TO CAUSE EVEN MORE HAVOC THAN USUAL.

A VICTORIAN TOWN HOUSE
London 1871

Proud of his home, proud of his family, proud of his nation and his own success, the owner of this house returns from the office where he works as a railway manager. His London home is not a castle nor an impressive country house, but it has the latest of everything. It is warm, comfortable and convenient. This is the home he feels he deserves, as a hardworking citizen of an empire that literally spans the globe.

Above: While cheaper houses are built in closely spaced, back-to-back rows, these grander homes, although still identical to each other, enjoy avenues and green spaces between them. Each square is planted as a small park, to be shared by the people living around it.

THE GROWING CITY

One of the guests being entertained to afternoon tea is amazed at the changes to this part of London. When she knew it ten years ago, there were fields here. Britain's success as an industrial nation and the technological advances that seem to happen every day mean that large numbers of houses can be built more quickly than ever before, by using machine-made components and a common plan for rows of homes. Even so, the population is increasing ever faster.

Above right: Just as in larger houses of the past, bells in the servants' quarters summon them when their services are needed.

Left: The Victorians have a genius for improvement and convenience. The postal service now means that letters can be delivered to the next street or the other side of the world more quickly than ever before, linking the far-flung corners of the British Empire.

EDUCATING FOR AN EMPIRE

The railway manager talks of the importance of education but he believes his sons and daughters have different needs. His sons are taught at home by a governess but will soon go away to school, where they will learn to take their place in the worlds of work and government. The governess teaches the girls, too, but they will stay at home and learn social and artistic accomplishments. They will marry and leave home or remain single and stay to look after aging parents.

Right: Factory-made tiles and sanitary ware make bathrooms quick to install and easy to clean. Piped hot water is a luxury undreamt of in earlier times.

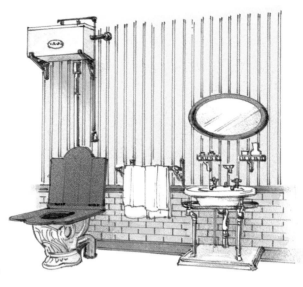

CLEANLINESS IS NEXT TO GODLINESS

This part of Victorian London is very different from the cramped, dirty slums described by novelists such as Dickens. Newer houses have been planned to make the most of advances in plumbing, heating and lighting. Clean water is piped into the house and efficient drains make this area more pleasant than some of the older, smellier ones! Gas for lighting is also piped into the house. It is cleaner and much safer than candles. Gas-lights outside have made the streets safer too.

UPSTAIRS AND DOWNSTAIRS

Although this is a home for just one family, keeping the house clean, cooking and looking after the children is still hard work. The railway manager has a good income and feels that a certain level of comfort is due to his position in life. For him, servants are easily affordable. Two maids and a cook, a nanny and a governess work here, although most of them do not live in.

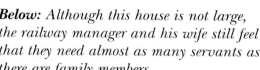

For the skivvy, the youngest maid, the day starts early and ends late. There is so much cleaning and dusting to do, mostly while the family is still in bed! How she wishes that this household did not enjoy filling every wall and shelf with paintings and ornaments, family photographs and ornate furniture – specially designed to trap dust!

Below: Although this house is not large, the railway manager and his wife still feel that they need almost as many servants as there are family members.

TODAY IN THE HOUSE...
TODAY A YOUNG SWEEP WHO HAS COME TO CLEAN THE CHIMNEYS FINDS HIMSELF MORE INVOLVED IN HIS WORK THAN USUAL, WHILE HIS MASTER IS ENTERTAINED ELSEWHERE IN THE HOUSE. A FOUR-FOOTED FRIEND MAY UNDO ALL THE WORK OF THE MAIDS WHO WERE CLEANING AT DAWN THIS MORNING!

FACTS & FEATURES

Location: the house is one of many identical ones, built around a square that all the occupiers can use.

Construction: the bricks, timber and wooden and plaster mouldings for this house have all been shaped by machine. The same components have been used in all the houses in this street, bringing down costs and speeding up building.

Dado rails: these rails run round the inside walls at waist height. They stop chair backs and other furniture from marking the wallpaper – but mean even more dusting for the maids!

Roofing slates: these have been brought over two hundred miles from Wales. Efficient roads, railways and canals make this possible and economical.

Pillars: on either side of the front door, pillar desgins "borrowed" from Greek and Roman times help to show that this is the home of an educated and cultured family.

Sash windows: the latest industrial methods make it possible for windows to contain large sheets of flawless glass, not the small panes of earlier times.

Railings: iron railings are also a sign of Britain's industrial power. It was the existence of iron ore and coal for smelting it in northern England that made the industrial revolution possible. Coal is used to heat this house too, and the much-used chimneys need frequent sweeping.

AN APARTMENT BLOCK
New York 1958

Since the end of the Second World War, things have been looking up in New York – in every sense of the word! As new opportunities, especially for young Americans, open up, people have flocked to the city. Building land on the island of Manhattan is some of the most expensive in the world. The answer is to build not out, but up! It is the only way to fit living spaces, offices and stores for thousands of people into one small area. None of this would be possible without machinery – enormous cranes now form an everyday part of the skyline.

ONE BUILDING, MANY HOMES

Like most large homes, the apartment block shelters many different kinds of people. In fact, ten families and some businesses are based here. But, although they may nod to each other in the lift, these people live separately, each group behind its own front door. In their own apartments, they have privacy to live their lives in different ways – as a peep inside immediately shows!

FAMILY LIFE

In the past, several generations of one large family would usually live together. Today, when travel and communications are so much easier, many homes are smaller, often consisting only of parents and two or three children. Without grand-parents to help around the house, one adult must stay at home to do all the jobs that servants and slaves would often have done in the past.

Electrical appliances that make cooking, washing and cleaning easier have become a necessity, not the luxury they once were. And for the first time, young people are leaving home before they marry, to share apart-ments and enjoy their own independence.

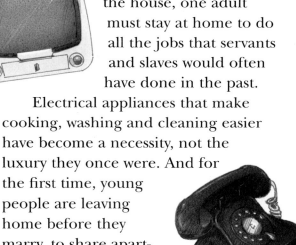

Above: As the buildings get taller and space for gardens in the city all but vanishes, Central Park becomes increasingly important as a green space that everyone can enjoy. That is vital in a city where concrete seems to be appearing wherever you look.

Left and right: Electrical machinery has transformed many everyday tasks. The machines are mass-produced in factories at low prices, ensuring that more and more people can afford to buy them. They are designed to be seen – in the kitchen or living room – to stand out as important items that show the success of the family that owns them.

SEPARATE BUT TOGETHER

Each family may be shut away privately in its own apartment, but it can still be sharing more than ever before with others. Every day television brings the same programmes into every-one's home. In cafés and bars, juke boxes play the same records all over the country. And the telephone makes it possible to speak instantly to a relative thousands of miles away or a friend in the next street. As news, travel and communications continue to improve, the world seems to be growing smaller by the day.

The elevator is the most likely meeting place for the families in this block, except today as it has broken down!

Top floor: *Apartments up here seem to be lived in by younger people. Perhaps they are less worried about days like this one, when there seems to be a problem with the lift – there are stairs as well, after all.*

Fifth floor: *With so many people in one building, sound-proofing is important. Even so, neighbours with young children dread the nights when there's a party.*

Fourth floor: *Maintenance of the well-used building is a never-ending task. No sooner have the painters finished on one floor than it is time to move on to the next. Of course, essential repairs always seem to happen at the most inconvenient times!*

Third floor: *This is a city where people are on the move all the time. It is not surprising that there always seems to be someone moving in or out of the building.*

Second floor: *In today's world everyone can enjoy the luxury of hot running water available throughout the day. People can choose to take a long, relaxing bath or a quick shower before dashing out.*

First floor: *With so many people on the move day and night, fast-food restaurants have a thriving business. The one in this block serves specialities from the many cultures that make up this neighbourhood.*

The basement: *This is the engine-room of the block. The heating boilers and electrical fuse boxes are located here. Washing machines cater for those who do not own their own. It is the janitor's job to keep this part of the building clean and functioning at all times, however difficult the task.*

TODAY IN THE APARTMENT BLOCK...
IN THE CITY THAT NEVER SLEEPS, SEVERAL PEOPLE ARE BEGINNING TO WISH THEY COULD, AFTER AN ALL-NIGHT PARTY.

FACTS & FEATURES

Location: in the heart of New York, the people in this apartment block can make use of all that the city has to offer. Almost anything can be delivered to the door after a brief phone call, and people whose families come from every part of the world bring their own traditions to this exciting centre.

Construction: engineers have calculated that brick is strong enough only for six storeys – as this building has. Increasingly, reinforced concrete and steel structures are able to rise much higher.

Elevator (lift): the introduction of an electrically powered lift means that living on the top floor of the block is as attractive as living on the first floor. Of course, lifts can break down, which stairs rarely do!

Lobby: as well as each family's private living space, there are public spaces in this building, looked after by a janitor. The lobby, stairs, laundry and lift are all used by everyone, but they still need to be kept clean and tidy.

Heating and plumbing: all the services that people could possibly need were considered when this building was designed. Electricity and water come into the building at one central point and are piped to each apartment. A massive boiler in the basement takes care of heating.

Keeping cool: this building is stifling in the hot New York summer, when fire exits are thrown open and people are glad to sit out in the cool of the evening. But at least refrigeration now means that food can be kept cool and fresh. That's important, with family members dashing in for meals at all hours.

31

INDEX